Vegan Coo

Delicious and Easy Recipes to Purify and Energize Your Body, Lose Weight Fast, and Be Happier Everyday

Written By

JANE BRACE

Table of Contents

The Avocado Melt 70

Chickenless Salad Sandwich 72

Lemongrass Tofu Banh Mi 74

PUDDINGS AND CUSTARDS 78

CREME BRULÈE 79

Chocolate Pudding 81

Pistachio Pudding 82

Vanilla Plum Rice Pudding 84

Tapioca Pudding 86

Fall Harvest Quinoa Pudding 87

Pumpkin Flan 89

Cremasicle Custard 91

Tiramisu 92

Brownie Batter Mousse 94

METRIC CONVERSIONS 97

BASICS

Health Nut (a.k.a. Nut Milk)

Lemon-aid

Spice of Life

Super Seed Me (a.k.a. Seed Milk)

Hawaiian Elixir (a.k.a. Pineapple Water)

Health Nut (a.k.a. Nut Milk)

❖

Since the dairy has been demonized by the health food industry, milk alternatives have been on the rise. However, most of the substitutes that have been adopted have some scary chemicals listed in their ingredients. Once you realize how easy it is to make them from scratch, you won't go back. When you include nut milk in juices and smoothies, the protein helps stabilize your blood sugar levels even if you add sweet fruits. Due to its high fat content, it takes longer to digest and keeps you full longer.

Makes 2½–3 cups

1 cup nuts, raw unsalted (any of these: almonds, pecans, hazelnuts, Brazil nuts, walnuts)

2 cups water

Put the nuts in a bowl, cover with water, and soak overnight. In the morning, drain the water and rinse the nuts. If they can be peeled (like almonds), it's better if you do it, as the skin is hard to digest. The peel should come off easily.

Process the nuts in a blender with 2 cups water, until they have completely liquefied. Pass through a sieve, pressing the solids that stay at the bottom with the back of a spoon, until no more liquid drips out of it. Refrigerate in an airtight container for up to 3 days, and stir well before using, because the tiny nut particles tend to accumulate at the bottom.

Lemon-aid

◆

It is common knowledge that drinking warm water with lemon after waking helps to purify the body.

Makes 1 glass

1 glass water (warm or at room temperature)

1 lemon

Squeeze the lemon into the water and drink immediately.

Spice of Life

This spicy water is an upgraded version of the powerfully cleansing water with lemon. Just add some warming and energizing ginger, a fiber source in the form of chia seeds, and a sprinkling of cayenne pepper. This wakes up your body's circulatory system.

Makes 1 glass

1-inch piece ginger, finely chopped
1 tablespoon chia seeds
Juice of 1 lime
A pinch of ground cayenne pepper
Put the ginger in a pan with 2 cups of water, and bring to a boil. Let it cool for a few minutes, and once it's lukewarm, remove the ginger, transfer to a glass, and add the chia seeds. Stir and soak for 5 minutes.

Add the lime juice, and sprinkle with cayenne pepper. Stir and serve.

Super Seed Me (a.k.a. Seed Milk)

When you make seed/nut milk you will be left with a bit of fiber after blending and straining it. You can use the fiber in bread or muffin recipes, add it to smoothies, sprinkle over breakfast or salads, or mix it with honey and yogurt for a wonderful homemade face and body scrub.

Makes 3 cups

⅓ cup sesame seeds

⅓ cup pumpkin seeds

⅓ cup sunflower seeds

2 cups water

Soak the seeds overnight in a bowl of water. In the morning, drain the water, and then process the seeds in a blender with 2 c. water, until you have a smooth liquid. Pass through a strainer, and press the remaining solids with a spoon to get all the water out of them. Store this milk in an airtight container in the fridge, for up to 3 days.

Hawaiian Elixir (a.k.a. Pineapple Water)

◆

This flavorful water is spicy, slightly sweet yet sugar free, and highly diuretic. Use it as the base for smoothies, or make it without the spices and grab a glass whenever you're thirsty to replace regular water. This is a great way to use pineapple peels instead of throwing them away.

Makes 4 cups

1 organic pineapple (skin only)

1 cinnamon stick

4 allspice berries

2 cloves

5 cups water

Clean the pineapple peel by scrubbing it with a brush under hot running water. Combine the pineapple peel, cinnamon, allspice, cloves, and 5 cups water in a

16

saucepan. Bring to a boil over medium heat and simmer for about 30 minutes. Turn off the heat and cool. Strain, discarding the solids. Transfer the pineapple water to a jar and keep refrigerated or at room temperature.

SUPER POWER GREENS

Cool as a Cucumber

Makes 1 glass

This juice is the epitome of coolness thanks to the light and refreshing effect of cucumbers and mint. Serve it over ice (or turn it into a slushy with crushed ice), and you have the secret weapon to survive any summer heat wave untouched.

½ cucumber

1 Granny Smith apple

1 kiwi, peeled

3 sprigs mint

1 cup parsley

½ lemon

Process all the ingredients in a juicer and serve.

Green Is In

If I had to recommend just one juice from our repertoire, this simple green recipe would perhaps be the winner. This drink is like a canvas for all the other fruits, vegetables, and superfoods lying around in your kitchen. And yes, you can think of yourself as the juice artist! Enjoy it as it is, or add whatever your body yearns for, making it new and exciting every time you drink it.

Makes 1 glass

½ cucumber

½ Granny Smith apple

2 celery ribs

½–1 heart of romaine

1–2 cups spinach, chard, or kale

Juice all the ingredients and serve.

Green apples have a lower glycemic index (GI) than most fruits, and that's why they're a great alternative to sweeten your juices. Including ingredients with a low GI in your juices will keep your blood sugar levels stable, which translates into fewer cravings, better mood, and higher levels of energy throughout the whole day.

Holy Kale

This juice is a great way to stock up on robust leafy greens without even noticing it. It has a pleasant parsley flavor with a lightly salted celery touch, and the sweetness of the carrots and apple are also present in every drop. Kale, however, goes almost unnoticed.

Makes 1 glass

1–2 carrots

2 kale leaves

4 lettuce leaves

½ cup parsley

½ Granny Smith apple

2 celery ribs

½ lemon

Process all the ingredients in a juicer and serve.

Carrots are ideal for juicing because they have a high water content and add their characteristic sweetness to any recipe. They will also strengthen your eyes and give your skin a beautiful golden tan in the summer that will be the envy of many. So stock up on them!

Simply Green

This is a much healthier pick-me-up than most commercial cereal bars or coffee. Notice that the recipe doesn't include any sweet fruits or veggies, which makes it your blood sugar's dream juice. A glass of it will alkalize your body, filling it with oxygen and giving your cells many of the essential nutrients they crave.

Makes 1 glass

½ cucumber

3 celery ribs

2 cups spinach

½–1 lime or lemon

Process all the ingredients in a juicer and serve.

This juice is so low in calories and sugar that you can drink it throughout the day to keep yourself hydrated. If you drink it often, it's better if you rotate the leafy greens and don't stick to the spinach every single time (chard, lettuce, and kale are other good alternatives). You can have too much of a good thing, and overdoing the same dark leafy greens all the time can have a toxic effect on some people.

Sweetchini

Surprisingly sweet, despite having only one sweet fruit listed among its ingredients, when you drink this you will be able to relax and enjoy the experience, while the juice does the rest.

Makes 1 glass

2 cups green beans

½–1 zucchini

½ lemon

1 apple

1 cup parsley

Juice all the ingredients and serve.

Herbs can be difficult to juice in certain juicers. One solution is to stop the juicer and throw a few pieces of fruit or veggies in it. Add a handful of herbs, and top with more fruits or veggies. Only then, turn the juicer on and start pressing. When sandwiched this way, tiny leaves and sprouts are more likely to yield juice.

Green Up

Broccoli doesn't have an unpleasant or strong flavor when added to juices. In fact, it has a slightly sweet effect. This sulfur-rich veggie helps the liver detoxification pathways work properly. Don't be shy and use every part of it: florets, stems, and leaves.

Makes 1 glass

1 cup broccoli

1 Granny Smith apple

1 cup pineapple

2 cups spinach

½-inch piece ginger, peeled

Put all the ingredients in a juicer, process, and serve.

A small amount of ginger in your juice can enhance many flavors and conceal others that you're not crazy about.

Healthy Mary

Forget hangovers, and welcome younger-looking skin, a slimmer body, more energy, and all-around awesomeness. This low-calorie savory juice will make you feel like you're always on vacation, sipping Bloody Marys in the middle of the day, but without any of the negative effects. Cheers to that!

Makes 1 glass

½ bell pepper

½ cucumber

½ zucchini

1 tomato

1 cup lettuce

½–1 lime

Dash of cayenne pepper

Process the bell pepper, cucumber, zucchini, tomato, lettuce, and lime in a juicer. Add a sprinkling of cayenne pepper, stir, and serve. You can put a celery stick in the glass for a real virgin Bloody Mary effect.

Legend has it that bell peppers are fabulous for the skin, and adding just a little piece of them to juices will give you a smooth and glowing complexion. Worth giving it a shot, don´t you think?

Green Raw-volution

Some health experts believe that the best time to have a replenishing drink like this is first thing in the morning. When you wake up, after several hours of natural "fasting" while you're sleeping, your body doesn't have any half-digested food blocking the road. A powerful green juice like this will breeze right into your bloodstream and cells.

Makes 1 glass

½ apple

½ orange

½ cucumber

1 cup kale

2 celery ribs

1 tablespoon chia seeds

Juice all the fruits and veggies. Add the chia seeds, stir, and let them soak for 5 to 10 minutes. If you don't use organic limes, lemons, or oranges, just squeeze them over your juices instead of going through the hassle of peeling them to pass them through the juicer. And don't forget the strainer! You don't want those sneaky little seeds falling into your pure and sparkling glass of juice.

Broccolini Genie

Juicing is simple: if it's green, you can be certain that it's good for you. But don't be misled into thinking that all green juices are the same and, hence, boring. There are all kinds of combinations you can come up with to bring some excitement into them every time. Broccolini is one of those unconventional options that will also help eliminate unwanted contaminants from your body.

Makes 1 glass

1 cup broccolini (florets and stems)
½ cucumber
4 celery ribs
1 ripe pear
½–1 lemon

Juice all the ingredients and serve.

When you juice broccoli, broccolini, or broccoli rabe, make sure you use the stalks and leaves too. People are too fast at throwing away the less attractive parts of fruits and veggies, unbeknownst to the fact that these are also packed with nutrients, sometimes even more so than the beautiful pulp or florets. This family of veggies shouldn't be juiced every single day, as they can become toxic if consumed too often.

I Love Radishes

Why stop at juicing sweet ingredients when you can also enjoy the pungency that radishes bring to every juice? These cute little veggies will help your liver become your body's worker of the month by providing many essential enzymes for its appropriate functioning. You can experiment with different kinds of radishes, such as daikon radish or black radish.

Makes 1 glass

1 cup zucchini

1 Granny Smith apple

1 small radish

1 cup broccoli

Juice of ½ lemon

Juice the first four ingredients. Squeeze in the lemon juice and serve.

If you go to the store or market and can't find the exact ingredients a recipe calls for, don't sweat it. It's easy to vary the ingredients in most juices. Here, for example, you can use cucumber or summer squash instead of zucchini, pear instead of apple, and lime or orange instead of lemon.

blood thinners, however, you should avoid drinking cranberry juice, as it can raise the blood levels of these drugs and become dangerous.

Makes 1 glass

1 cup cranberries

1 apple

2 celery ribs

1 cup spinach

½ cucumber

½ cup cilantro

Process all the ingredients in a juicer and serve.

Serious Business

This drink has the exact taste one would expect from a green juice: mild, slightly sweet, with a hint of spice. The peppery flavor is given by mustard greens, a leafy green that we haven't used nearly as much as we should have in this book, because its taste may be too strong for many people. This juice, however, shows how to do it right, enhancing its flavor instead of overpowering it.

Makes 1 glass

½ cucumber

½ cup broccoli

½ Granny Smith apple

2 celery ribs

½ cup spinach

1 cup escarole

1 mustard green leaf

Process all the ingredients in a juicer and serve.

The strong personality of mustard greens matches their strong healing power. They lower cholesterol (especially when cooked), and are rich in phytonutrients that help prevent cancer. They are kick-ass detoxifying and anti-inflammatory agents, and they are also full of antioxidants.

Heart Chakra

The heart chakra is known to be the energetic center of our immune system. It also happens to be green, and is enhanced by any contact with green colors. No wonder green juices are so good for health! Whenever you need to heal any part of your body, you can concentrate on your heart center, and imagine green light being sent from there to the affected area. Romaine lettuce increases the vitamin and mineral content of juices and smoothies. This leafy veggie should be your best friend if you're looking to lose weight, and you can have as much as you want because its calories are few.

Makes 1 glass

2 mustard green leaves

2 kiwis, peeled

½ heart of romaine

½ zucchini

1 cup broccoli

½ lemon

½ cup blueberries

Process all the ingredients in a juicer and serve.

Southern Soul

Just like mustard greens, collard greens help lower cholesterol and are an anticancer powerhouse. Strong-flavored leafy greens like these two examples are detoxifying, antioxidant, and anti-inflammatory, so include them in your diet (and your juices) as often as you can. You can learn to like them—if you don't already—by starting to consume them little by little.

Makes 1 glass

1 cup collard greens
½ cup parsley
1 cup lettuce
½ cucumber
½ orange
1 carrot
2 celery ribs
Process all the ingredients in a juicer and serve.

You may have noticed that most of our juices have a cucumber base. This veggie is mother nature's offering to juicers, as it has buckets of water and goes well with mostly anything. Chinese medicine uses it to dissipate heat, and as a diuretic, laxative, and detoxifying aid.

Beet the Blues

If you're an eighties kid, the color of this juice may bring back memories of grape-flavored chewing gum rolls that came in hard plastic containers. Thankfully, in this case the cheerful color is not the result of scary chemicals and colorings, but of all the goodness stored inside blueberries and beets instead. When using beets, don't discard the greens. They are as good as the roots, and have a similar earthy flavor. In fact, beets were originally grown for their leaves, not their roots. You can use yellow or white beets, but nothing is more stunning than the intense magenta color that regular beets give to any juice.

Makes 1 glass

½–1 beet (with leaves, optional)

1 cup blueberries

½ heart of romaine

2 celery ribs

½–1 cucumber

½ apple

½-inch piece ginger, peeled

Process all the ingredients in a juicer and serve.

Beet-er Dandelion

This intensely colored and flavored juice is not for the fainthearted. The bitterness of dandelion may put sweetness seekers off this drink, but for me, its superior detoxifying properties more than make up for it. No pain, no gain. If you want the real hardcore version of this juice, have it without the apple. The beets and carrots already are rich in sugar, and more fruit only adds to it. However, if you really need it, you can add the fruit to get the benefits of the dandelion leaves past your taste buds.

Makes 1 glass

2 dandelion leaves

1 beet

1 carrot

½ cucumber

½–1 lemon

½ Granny Smith apple (optional)

Juice all the ingredients and serve.

Save the Veggies

Tomatoes are part of the nightshade group of foods, which have somewhat of a bad rep for having toxins that cause inflammation and pain. Defenders of nightshades, which also include potatoes, peppers, and eggplants, claim that the benefits far outweigh any potential problems caused by such low doses of these toxins. Our verdict? As long as you're not overdoing it, you can reap positive benefits from mostly anything.

Makes 1 glass

1 cup berries

1 tomato

1–2 cups spinach

½–1 cup pineapple water

Juice the first three ingredients. Mix with the pineapple water and serve.

Forever Young

The strong cilantro flavor in this refreshing juice is perfectly balanced by the sweetness of the carrots and the acidity of the lemon. The result is a truly enjoyable drink that will flush a huge amount of toxins out of your body. This is a recipe you may want to go back to again and again, not only for how much your liver loves it, but also for how much you do.

Makes 1 glass

½ cucumber

1 large carrot

1 cup cilantro

Juice of ½ lemon

Juice the cucumber, carrots, and cilantro. Squeeze the lemon into the juice and stir.

The Tummy Rub

This green juice is an efficient cleanser and tonic of the hardworking yet delicate digestive system. Drink it half an hour before a heavy meal, as it stimulates your gut and gets it ready for action. You can also replace a meal with it if you're feeling heavy from a previous binge. Fennel has an aniseed flavor and, similar to that seed, aids digestion and prevents gas. It is also known to be a diuretic, reduce inflammation, and prevent cancer. As a food, only the round bulb is usually used, but for juicing use the bulb, stalks, and leaves. Everything goes.

Makes 1 glass

1 cup pineapple chunks
½ fennel bulb
½ cucumber
1 cup spinach
½ lemon

Process all the ingredients in a juicer and serve.

Cheers to Watercress

The strong peppery taste of watercress has the spotlight in this juice, warming up your throat and stomach when you drink it. We rather enjoy it, although this may be too edgy for those who consider sweetness to be the only acceptable taste in a juice. Be brave and have it as a shot one day, or every day. If you like it, go ahead and have a whole glass (you may have to triple the recipe to get a decent-sized glass of it). Watercress is an ace at detoxifying the liver and cleansing the blood. It is also a master antibiotic, improves eye health and night blindness, keeps your bones healthy, and prevents several kinds of cancer. Toast for health with this instead of booze, and you will be doing your liver a big favor.

Makes 1 shot

½ cup watercress

½ cup cucumber

½ cup carrot

¼ lime, peeled

Juice all the ingredients and serve in a shot glass.

Salad in a Glass

The color of this juice is as deep as the level of well-being it will bring to the new and improved you. Juice it once and your body will feel the difference. Juice it more often and you and everyone around you will notice its powerful effect. Boasting large amounts of sulfur, calcium, magnesium, iron, and vitamins, broccoli is a superb ingredient to include in juices and smoothies. Choose dark green heads and store them in the fridge inside a plastic bag to keep them from getting limp. Always try to use them before they start turning yellow.

Makes 1 glass

1 cup broccoli
1 cup spinach
1 beet
1 apple
½ cucumber
½-inch piece ginger, peeled
Process all the ingredients in a juicer and serve.

Happy Belly

If you like an aromatic hint in your juice, this recipe is for you. Some people dislike the flavors of anise, licorice, fennel, and the like, but if they knew what wonderful digestive aids these are, maybe they would change their minds. Like in tomatoes, the red color of watermelons are the result of their high lycopene content, which makes them especially important for the heart.

Makes 1 glass

½ fennel bulb

1 cup watermelon, cubed and seeded

1 cup zucchini

1 cup spinach

1 cup parsley

½ lemon

Process all the ingredients in a juicer and serve.

Juice and Be Merry

Beets are one of the most detoxifying foods under the sun, as they are powerful cleansers of the bladder, kidneys, and liver. Anytime is good to have a tall glass of fresh beet juice, but take it one beet at a time as you build up your cleansing stamina. Some cucumbers you buy at the grocery store may come covered in a thin layer of wax. You will have to take a close look to notice it, because it's transparent. When making juice, make sure you peel your cucumbers if they're not organic and if they have this waxy outer skin.

Makes 1 glass

1 beet

1 apple

2 celery ribs

½ cucumber

½–1 lemon

Process all the ingredients in a juicer and serve.

Yellow Submarine

If you are having digestive issues and have tried everything without results, this may be your lucky day. Cabbage and pineapple work wonders for your body's oven, helping with uncomfortable issues like indigestion and heartburn. You won't even need to cover your nose to drink the sometimes intimidating cabbage juice, as the dominating sweetness of pineapple will come to the rescue. Despite its pale complexion, which makes it look not so interesting or potent, cabbage is very rich in sulfur, an antioxidant that is greatly detoxifying for the liver and increases the production of bile.

Makes 1 glass

2 cups cabbage

1 cup pineapple chunks

½ cucumber

Process all the ingredients in a juicer and serve.

VEGANIZED FAMILY FAVORITES

Tempeh Sausage Minestrone

SERVES 8 TO 10

PREP TIME: 35 minutes
ACTIVE TIME: 25 minutes (not including time to make Quick Sausage Crumbles)
INACTIVE TIME: 20 minutes

1 tablespoon olive oil

½ red onion, diced

2 medium carrots, peeled and sliced

2 celery stalks, sliced

½ fennel bulb, diced

2 cups sliced cremini mushrooms (or button mushrooms)

2 cups broccoli florets

2 small yellow squash, halved lengthwise and sliced

One 28-ounce can no-salt-added diced tomatoes

5 cups low-sodium vegetable broth

5 cups water

3 tablespoons liquid aminos (or gluten-free tamari; use coconut aminos to be soy-free)

2 teaspoons dried basil

2 teaspoons dried thyme

2 teaspoons dried oregano

½ teaspoon paprika

¼ teaspoon cayenne pepper

2 cups pasta (gluten-free if necessary)

1½ cups cooked great Northern beans (or one 15-ounce can, rinsed and drained)

1 cup frozen green peas

Quick Sausage Crumbles

2 cups packed chopped kale (or chard)

Salt and black pepper to taste

1. Heat the olive oil in your largest pot. Add the onion and sauté until the onion is just becoming translucent. Add the carrot, celery, fennel, and mushrooms and sauté for 2 to 3 minutes. Add the broccoli, squash, tomatoes and their liquid, broth, water, liquid aminos, basil, thyme, oregano, paprika, and cayenne pepper and bring to a boil. Reduce to a simmer and cook for about 10 minutes.

2. Add the pasta, beans, and peas and simmer until the pasta is al dente, about 10 minutes. Add the sausage crumbles, kale, salt, and pepper. Remove from the heat and serve immediately. Leftovers will keep in an airtight container in the fridge for 5 to 6 days, or frozen for up to 2 months.

Pot-obello Roast

PREP TIME: 20 minutes
ACTIVE TIME: 35 minutes   **INACTIVE TIME:** 20 minutes

4 large portobello mushrooms

1 tablespoon olive oil

1 small red onion, quartered

6 shallots, trimmed and halved lengthwise

2 tablespoons brown rice flour (or other flour)

¼ cup vegan red wine

2 tablespoons liquid aminos (or gluten-free tamari; use coconut aminos to be soy-free)

1 tablespoon vegan Worcestershire sauce (gluten-free and/or soy-free if necessary)

1 teaspoon dried parsley

1 teaspoon salt

1 teaspoon black pepper

½ teaspoon paprika

3 cups vegan low-sodium "no-beef" flavored broth (or regular vegetable broth)

1 tablespoon nutritional yeast

1 pound small carrots, peeled (or baby carrots)

1 pound fingerling potatoes, halved lengthwise

8 ounces brussels sprouts, halved

4 thyme sprigs

2 rosemary sprigs

1. Remove the stems from the mushrooms and chop the stems into bite-size pieces. Set the stems and caps aside separately.

2. Preheat the oven to 400°F . Heat the oil in a large oven-safe pot or Dutch oven over medium heat. Add the onion and shallots and sauté for about 5 minutes, until softened. Add the flour and cook, stirring, until the flour is not visible, 1 to 2 minutes. Add the wine, liquid aminos, Worcestershire sauce, parsley, salt, pepper, and paprika and cook, stirring, for 2 to 3 minutes, until the mixture has thickened. Add the broth and stir in the nutritional yeast. Add the chopped mushroom stems, carrots, potatoes, and brussels sprouts and bring to a boil. Reduce the heat to a simmer and cook for about 5 minutes.

3. Remove from the heat. Arrange the portobello mushroom caps in the center of the pan, with vegetables surrounding and under them, and spoon sauce over the tops until well covered. Top with the thyme and rosemary sprigs. Cover the pot and place it in the oven. Roast for 15 minutes, then remove the lid and roast for another 5 minutes, uncovered. The mushrooms and vegetables should all be very tender. Remove from the oven.

4. You can serve straight from the pot, or arrange the portobello caps in the center of a platter surrounded by the vegetables and garnished with the herbs, and spoon the sauce over the top. Leftovers will keep in an airtight container in the fridge for 2 to 3 days.

Sweet Potato Casserole

SERVES 8

PREP TIME: 20 minutes
ACTIVE TIME: 25 minutes
INACTIVE TIME: 20 minutes

casserole

4 pounds sweet potatoes or yams, peeled and roughly chopped

Vegan cooking spray (soy-free if necessary)

⅓ cup unsweetened nondairy milk (soy-free if necessary)

⅓ cup maple syrup

¼ cup coconut sugar (or brown sugar)

3 tablespoons vegan butter (soy-free if necessary; or coconut oil), melted

2 tablespoons lemon juice

1 tablespoon nutritional yeast, optional

1 teaspoon ground cinnamon

½ teaspoon ground ginger

½ teaspoon salt

¼ teaspoon ground nutmeg

topping

1½ cups chopped pecans

1 cup rolled oats (certified gluten-free if necessary)

1 cup vegan cornflakes (certified gluten-free if necessary)

⅓ cup oat flour (certified gluten-free if necessary)

¼ cup coconut sugar (or brown sugar)

1 teaspoon ground cinnamon

¼ teaspoon salt

4 tablespoons vegan butter (soy-free if necessary; or coconut oil), melted

1 tablespoon maple syrup

1. To make the casserole : Place the sweet potatoes in a large pot and cover with water. Bring to a boil and cook for 8 to 10 minutes, until tender. Remove from the heat and drain. Set aside.

2. Preheat the oven to 350°F. Lightly spray a 9 × 13-inch baking dish with cooking spray.

3. Transfer the sweet potatoes to a large bowl. Add the milk, maple syrup, sugar, butter, lemon juice, nutritional yeast (if using), cinnamon, ginger, salt, and nutmeg. Use a masher to mash and combine the mixture until mostly smooth. Transfer to the prepared baking dish.

4. To make the topping : Mix together the pecans, oats, cornflakes, oat flour, sugar, cinnamon, and salt. Pour the melted butter and maple syrup over the top and stir until combined. Spread the topping over the casserole.

5. Bake for 20 minutes, or until the topping is crispy and the casserole is heated through. Serve immediately. Leftovers will keep in an airtight container in the fridge for 3 to 4 days.

VARIATION For a richer flavor, instead of boiling the sweet potatoes, roast them whole for 1 hour at 400°F . Let them cool, then scoop the flesh from the skins.

Skillet Cornbread

SERVES 8

PREP TIME: 5 minutes
ACTIVE TIME: 15 minutes
INACTIVE TIME: 35 minutes

Olive oil spray (or vegan cooking spray, soy-free if necessary)

1 cup unsweetened almond milk

1 teaspoon apple cider vinegar

¼ cup + 2 tablespoons warm water

2 tablespoons flax meal

1½ cups fine cornmeal (certified gluten-free if necessary)

1 cup oat flour (certified gluten-free if necessary)

¼ cup almond flour

1 tablespoon baking powder

½ teaspoon salt

½ teaspoon ground cumin

¼ teaspoon smoked paprika

¼ cup sunflower oil (or grapeseed oil)

¼ cup maple syrup

1. Preheat the oven to 400°F . Spray a 10-inch cast-iron skillet with olive oil.

2. In a 2-cup liquid measuring cup or a medium bowl, combine the milk with the vinegar. In a small cup or bowl, mix together the water and flax meal. Let both rest while you prepare the rest of the ingredients, or for 3 to 4 minutes

3. In a large bowl, whisk together the cornmeal, oat flour, almond flour, baking powder, salt, cumin, and paprika.

4. Once the flax meal mixture has thickened, add it to the milk. Add the sunflower oil and maple syrup. Stir until fully combined.

5. Add the wet ingredients to the dry ingredients and stir until just combined. Pour into the prepared skillet.

6. Bake for 20 to 25 minutes, until a toothpick inserted into the center comes out clean. Let rest for 5 to 10 minutes before serving. Leftovers will keep in an airtight container in the fridge for 2 to 3 days.

Grandma's Famous Date Nut Bread

MAKES 1 LOAF, 12 SLICES

PREP TIME: 15 minutes
ACTIVE TIME: 15 minutes
INACTIVE TIME: 75 minutes

1 cup chopped pitted dates

¾ cup chopped walnuts

1½ teaspoons baking soda

½ teaspoon salt

⅛ teaspoon xanthan gum (exclude if using all-purpose flour or if your gluten-free blend includes it)

¾ cup boiling water

3 tablespoons vegan butter (soy-free if necessary)

Vegan cooking spray (soy-free if necessary)

½ cup unsweetened applesauce

1 tablespoon apple cider vinegar

1 teaspoon vanilla extract

1½ cups unbleached all-purpose flour (or gluten-free flour blend, soy-free if necessary)

1 cup coconut sugar (or brown sugar)

1. Combine the dates, walnuts, baking soda, salt, and xanthan gum (if using) in a medium bowl. Pour in the boiling water and stir in the butter. Let the mixture rest for 20 minutes.

2. Preheat the oven to 350°F. Spray a 9 × 5-inch loaf pan with cooking spray.

3. In a large bowl, stir together the applesauce, vinegar, and vanilla. Gradually stir in the flour and sugar. It will be lumpy, and that's okay; just incorporate everything as thoroughly as you can. Add the date mixture and stir until combined. Pour into the prepared loaf pan.

4. Bake for 50 to 55 minutes, until a toothpick inserted in the center comes out clean. Let cool in the pan for 15 minutes before transferring to a cooling rack. Cool for at least 4 hours before slicing. Leftovers can be stored in an airtight container at room temperature for 3 to 4 days.

Peanut Butter Pie

MAKES 8 SLICES

PREP TIME: 10 minutes (not including time to chill coconut cream)
ACTIVE TIME: 25 minutes   INACTIVE TIME: 2 hours + 10 minutes

Vegan cooking spray (soy-free if necessary)

crust

1 cup oat flour (certified gluten-free if necessary)

½ cup almond flour

¼ cup coconut sugar (or brown sugar)

1 tablespoon arrowroot powder

1 teaspoon ground cinnamon

½ teaspoon vanilla powder, optional

½ teaspoon baking soda

½ teaspoon salt

6 tablespoons very cold vegan butter (soy-free if necessary)

1 teaspoon apple cider vinegar

filling

1 cup unsalted, unsweetened, smooth natural peanut butter

One 12-ounce vacuum-packed block extra firm silken tofu

5 tablespoons chilled, hardened canned coconut cream (see Tip)

½ cup coconut sugar (or brown sugar)

2 tablespoons tapioca powder

1 teaspoon vanilla extract

½ teaspoon salt

peanut butter crumble

¼ cup unsalted, unsweetened, smooth natural peanut butter

¼ cup oat flour (certified gluten-free if necessary)

¼ cup powdered sugar (or xylitol)

1. Preheat the oven to 375°F . Lightly spray a 9-inch pie pan with cooking spray.

2. To make the crust : In a large bowl, whisk together the oat flour, almond flour, sugar, arrowroot, cinnamon, vanilla powder (if using), baking soda, and salt. Cut in the butter and vinegar until it has the texture of wet sand and no pieces are larger than your pinkie fingernail.

3. Pour the mixture into the pie pan and use your hands to evenly distribute and spread the crust along the bottom and up the sides. Bake for 10 minutes. Remove from the oven and let cool completely before adding the filling.

4. To make the filling : In a food processor, combine the peanut butter, tofu, coconut cream, sugar, tapioca powder, vanilla, and salt. Process until smooth. Pour into the prepared crust. Refrigerate until ready to use.

5. To make the crumble : In a small bowl, combine the ingredients and stir with a fork until crumbly. Sprinkle the crumbles over the top of the pie. Chill for at least 2 hours, or until ready to serve. Leftovers will keep in an airtight container in the fridge for 1 to 2 days.

TIP Refrigerate a can of coconut cream or full-fat coconut milk overnight. The cream will harden and separate from the water. Use a can opener to open the can and lift off the lid. Carefully spoon out the solid coconut cream. Discard the water (or save it for later use). If you can find a 5.4-ounce can coconut cream, it will provide you with all the cream you need for this recipe.

VEGAN SANDWICHES

Fillet o' Chickpea Sandwich with Tartar Sauce Slaw

MAKES 6 SANDWICHES

PREP TIME: 25 minutes (not including time to cook brown rice and make Basic Cashew Cheese Sauce)
ACTIVE TIME: 50 minutes
INACTIVE TIME: 2 hours

tartar sauce

½ cup raw cashews, soaked in warm water for 1 hour and drained, water reserved

¼ cup reserved soaking water

¼ cup vegan mayonnaise (soy-free if necessary)

¼ cup lemon juice

1 tablespoon caper brine

1 teaspoon dried dill

slaw

3 cups shredded cabbage

1 cup grated carrot

chickpea fillets

1½ cups cooked chickpeas (or one 15-ounce can, rinsed and drained)

1 tablespoon liquid aminos (use coconut aminos to be soy-free)

One 14- to 15-ounce can artichoke hearts, rinsed and drained

1 cup cooked brown rice

¼ cup + 1 tablespoon chickpea flour, plus more if needed

1 tablespoon Old Bay Seasoning

½ to 1 teaspoon kelp granules

½ teaspoon dried dill

Salt and black pepper to taste

1½ cups vegan bread crumbs (gluten-free if necessary)

Vegetable oil for pan-frying

sandwiches

Basic Cashew Cheese Sauce

6 vegan sandwich rolls or burger buns (gluten-free if necessary), split horizontally

Sliced avocado

1. **To make the tartar sauce** : Combine the tartar sauce ingredients in a food processor or blender and process until smooth.

2. **To make the slaw** : Combine the shredded cabbage and carrots in a large bowl and add ½ cup of the tartar sauce. Mix until fully combined and chill for at least 1 hour. Transfer the remaining tartar sauce to a small bowl and refrigerate until needed.

3. **To make the chickpea fillets** : Heat a large frying pan, preferably cast iron, over medium heat. Add the chickpeas and cook for a couple of minutes. Add the liquid aminos and cook for 5 to 7 minutes, stirring occasionally, until the liquid has been absorbed. Remove from the heat. Use a fork or pastry cutter to gently mash the chickpeas. You only have to mash them a bit; you still want them a little chunky.

4. Place the artichoke hearts in a food processor and pulse 5 to 7 times, until the artichokes are broken down into little pieces but not mushy.

5. Combine the chickpeas, artichokes, rice, and chickpea flour in a large bowl. Use your hands to mash the mixture until it's fully combined and will hold together when you squeeze it. If it doesn't hold together, add more chickpea flour by the tablespoon until it holds. Add the Old Bay, kelp granules to taste, the dill, salt, and pepper and mix until combined.

6. Line a baking sheet with parchment paper or a silicone baking mat. Line a plate with paper towels to drain the cooked fillets.

7. Pour the bread crumbs into a shallow bowl. Divide the chickpea mixture into six equal portions. One at a time, shape each into the fillet shape of your choice (round, square, rectangle), place in the bread crumbs, and gently flip until all sides are covered. Gently shake off the excess crumbs and place on the prepared baking sheet.

8. Heat a large frying pan over medium heat. Add oil until the bottom of the pan is thinly coated. Once the oil begins to shimmer, add 2 or 3 fillets. Cook for 2 to 3 minutes on each side, until both sides are golden. Transfer the fillets to the paper-towel-lined plate to drain the excess oil. Cover with a clean kitchen cloth to keep warm while you repeat with the remaining filets (adding more oil to the pan if necessary).

9. To assemble each sandwich : Spread cheese on the bottom half of a roll and spread tartar sauce on the top half. Place a fillet on top of the cheese sauce, then add some avocado slices, a pile of slaw, and cover with the top half of the roll. Serve immediately. If you plan to eat the sandwich later, store it in an airtight container and refrigerate for up 5 hours. Leftover fillets will keep in an airtight container in the fridge for 3 to 4 days.

The Portobello Philly Reuben

MAKES 4 SANDWICHES

PREP TIME: 15 minutes (not including time to make Smoked Gouda Cheese Sauce)

ACTIVE TIME: 20 minutes **INACTIVE TIME: 10 minutes**

Russian dressing

⅓ cup vegan mayonnaise (soy-free if necessary)

1 tablespoon ketchup

1 tablespoon no-salt-added tomato paste

2 teaspoons red wine vinegar

1 teaspoon dried dill

½ teaspoon smoked paprika

2 to 3 tablespoons sweet pickle relish

sandwiches

4 portobello mushroom caps

Olive oil spray

2 tablespoons liquid aminos (or gluten-free tamari; use coconut aminos to be soy-free)

2 tablespoons vegan Worcestershire sauce (gluten-free and/or soy-free if necessary)

Black pepper to taste

4 vegan sandwich rolls (gluten-free if necessary), split horizontally

Smoked Gouda Cheese Sauce, _Melty Variation_

Loads of sauerkraut

1. To make the Russian dressing : Stir together the mayonnaise, ketchup, tomato paste, vinegar, dill, and paprika in a small bowl. Add relish to taste. Chill until ready to use.

2. To make the sandwiches : Preheat the oven to 425°F. Line a baking sheet with parchment paper or a silicone baking mat. Lightly spray the top and bottom of each portobello cap with olive oil and place on the baking sheet gill side up.

3. In a small cup or bowl, mix together the liquid aminos and Worcestershire sauce. Drizzle over the mushrooms, then sprinkle with pepper. Bake for 10 minutes. Remove from the oven and let cool for a few minutes. Slice the mushrooms on a bias into ½-inch strips. Heat the cheese sauce and keep warm.

4. Preheat the broiler. Arrange the rolls on the baking sheet, cut side up. Lay portobello strips on the bottom halves. Spread or drop cheese sauce on top of the mushrooms. Place under the broiler for 1 to 2 minutes, until the cheese is golden and the bread is toasted.

5. Add a pile of sauerkraut onto the cheesy half of each sandwich, then spread Russian dressing on the top half of each roll. Place the top half on top of the sandwich and serve immediately.

BBQ Pulled Jackfruit Sandwich

MAKES 4 SANDWICHES

PREP TIME: 10 minutes (not including time to make Creamy, Crunchy Coleslaw)
ACTIVE TIME: 20 minutes
INACTIVE TIME: 20 minutes

BBQ jackfruit

One 20-ounce can jackfruit (packed in brine or water, not syrup)

1 teaspoon olive oil

½ sweet onion, chopped

1 garlic clove, minced

½ teaspoon ground cumin

½ teaspoon smoked paprika

¾ cup vegan barbecue sauce (homemade or store-bought)

1 to 2 tablespoons sriracha

2 teaspoons arrowroot powder

Salt and black pepper to taste

sandwiches

4 vegan sandwich rolls or burger buns (gluten-free if necessary), split horizontally

Creamy, Crunchy Coleslaw

Sliced avocado, optional

1. Preheat the oven to 400°F . Line a baking sheet with parchment paper or a silicone baking mat.

2. Rinse and drain the jackfruit. Use two forks or your fingers to pull it apart into shreds, so that it somewhat resembles pulled meat. It will fall apart even more when you cook it.

3. Heat the oil in a large shallow saucepan over medium heat. Add the onion and garlic and sauté until the onion is translucent. Add the jackfruit, cumin, and paprika and cook, stirring occasionally, for about 5 minutes. Add salt and pepper.

4. In a cup or small bowl, stir together the barbecue sauce, sriracha, and arrowroot powder. Add to the jackfruit. Cook for 1 minute.

5. Spread out the jackfruit on the prepared baking sheet. Bake for 20 minutes, stirring once halfway through, until sauce is thick and sticky.

6. **To assemble the sandwich** : Open a roll on a plate. Place avocado slices (if using) on the bottom half. Scoop a heap of the jackfruit on top, then top the jackfruit with a pile of coleslaw. Place the other half of the roll on top and serve immediately. Leftover jackfruit will keep in an airtight container in the fridge for 3 to 4 days.

The Avocado Melt

PREP TIME: 15 minutes (not including time to Basic Cashew Cheese Sauce)
ACTIVE TIME: 10 minutes

4 bread slices (gluten-free if necessary)

Vegan butter (soy-free if necessary)

1 avocado, pitted, peeled, and sliced

Salt and black pepper to taste

½ batch Basic Cashew Cheese Sauce, _Melty Variation_ (see Tip)

Optional add-ins: _Quick Bacon Crumbles_, _Pickled Red Cabbage & Onion Relish_, sliced tomatoes, chopped green onions

Vegan mayonnaise (soy-free if necessary)

1. Preheat the broiler.

2. Toast the bread in a toaster on a medium setting—you don't want it to get too toasted. Lightly butter the toast. Spread out half of the avocado slices on each of two slices of toast. Place both on a baking sheet. Sprinkle salt and pepper over the avocado. Drizzle or dollop cheese sauce on top. Place the baking sheet under the broiler for about 2 minutes, until the cheese is lightly browned. Remove from

the oven and top with your desired add-ins (if using). Spread mayonnaise on the remaining slices of toast and place them on top of the sandwiches. Serve immediately.

TIP

Heat the cheese sauce right before you're ready to put the sandwiches in the oven.

Chickenless Salad Sandwich

MAKES 4 SANDWICHES

PREP TIME: 15 minutes

ACTIVE TIME: 15 minutes   INACTIVE TIME: 1 hour + 50 minutes

½ cup low-sodium "no-chicken" flavored vegetable broth (or regular low-sodium vegetable broth)

¼ cup liquid aminos (or gluten-free tamari; use coconut aminos to be soy-free)

1 teaspoon dried thyme

½ teaspoon dried marjoram

½ teaspoon garlic powder

½ teaspoon onion powder

½ teaspoon paprika

½ teaspoon liquid smoke

One 14-ounce block extra firm tofu, drained and pressed for 1 hour (see How to Press Tofu)

⅓ cup vegan mayonnaise

1 teaspoon Dijon mustard (gluten-free if necessary)

1 teaspoon dried dill

2 celery stalks, halved lengthwise and finely chopped

¼ small yellow onion, diced

Salt and black pepper to taste

Lettuce

Sliced tomato

8 vegan bread slices (or 4 vegan sandwich rolls; gluten-free if necessary)

1. Combine the broth, liquid aminos, thyme, marjoram, garlic powder, onion powder, paprika, and liquid smoke in an 8 × 8-inch baking dish. Slice the tofu into ½-inch cubes, add to the marinade, and toss until coated. Marinate the tofu for 20 minutes, tossing a couple of times to evenly distribute the marinade.

2. Preheat the oven to 350°F. Line a baking sheet with parchment paper or a silicone baking mat. Use a slotted spoon to scoop and spread the tofu onto the prepared baking sheet. Bake for 30 minutes, tossing once halfway through, until crisp and golden brown. Remove the tofu from the oven and let cool for about 5 minutes.

3. Combine the mayonnaise, mustard, and dill in a large bowl. Add the celery, onion, and tofu and stir until thoroughly combined. Season with salt and pepper. You can eat it right away or chill it before serving to allow the flavors to marry. The salad can be made up to 2 days before serving.

4. To assemble each sandwich, place some lettuce and sliced tomato on one bread slice (or the bottom half of a roll). Add a big pile of the salad and top with another slice of bread or the top of the roll. Serve immediately, or store the sandwiches in an airtight container in the fridge for up to 5 hours.

Lemongrass Tofu Banh Mi

MAKES 2 LARGE OR 4 SMALL SANDWICHES, WITH EXTRA SALAD

PREP TIME: 25 minutes
ACTIVE TIME: 25 minutes
INACTIVE TIME: 24 hours

pickled carrot & daikon salad

1 cup julienned carrot

1 cup julienned daikon radish

1 small jalapeño, sliced

½ cup water

¼ cup rice vinegar

2 tablespoons agave syrup

¼ teaspoon salt

lemongrass tofu

One 14-ounce block extra firm tofu, drained and pressed for at least 30 minutes (see How to Press Tofu)

4 lemongrass stalks, ends trimmed and outer leaves discarded, roughly chopped

1 garlic clove, minced

2 tablespoons water

2 tablespoons gluten-free tamari

1 tablespoon lemon juice

1 teaspoon maple syrup

1 teaspoon sriracha

1 teaspoon liquid smoke

1 tablespoon coconut oil

2 tablespoons sesame seeds, optional

sriracha aïoli

½ cup vegan mayonnaise

1 or 2 garlic cloves, minced and pressed

2 tablespoons lemon juice

1 tablespoon sriracha

sandwiches

1 long vegan baguette (or 2 large or 4 small vegan sandwich rolls; gluten-free if necessary), split horizontally

1 cup thinly sliced cucumber

Chopped fresh cilantro

Sliced jalapeño

Chopped green onions (green and white parts)

1. A day prior to serving, **make the salad** : Combine the carrot and daikon with the jalapeño in a large jar or other airtight container. Stir together the water, vinegar, agave syrup, and salt in a large measuring cup. Pour the brine over the veggies and cover with a tight-fitting lid. Shake the container to fully mix everything together, then refrigerate for at least 1 day. It will keep for 2 weeks.

2. To make the lemongrass tofu : Chop the tofu in half both ways, making four rectangles. Combine the lemongrass, garlic, water, tamari, lemon juice, maple syrup, sriracha, and liquid smoke in a blender. Blend until smooth. If necessary, add more water by the tablespoon to thin it into a sauce. Pour into an 8 × 8-inch baking dish. Place the tofu rectangles in the baking dish and turn over so both sides are covered in the marinade. Let the tofu marinate for 20 minutes, flipping them once halfway through.

3. While the tofu is marinating, **make the aïoli** : Combine all the ingredients in a small cup or bowl, stirring until well mixed.

4. After the tofu has finished marinating, heat the coconut oil in a large frying pan, preferably cast iron, over medium heat. Add the tofu rectangles and cook for 2 to 3 minutes per side, until each side has a crispy, golden exterior. Drizzle half of the leftover marinade into the pan and cook the tofu for 1 minute more, or until the liquid has been absorbed. Flip the tofu, add the remaining marinade, and cook until the liquid has been absorbed. Add the sesame seeds and toss until coated. Remove from the heat.

5. Slice the rounded ends off the baguette, then cut it in half to make two large sandwiches or into four pieces for small sandwiches.

6. To assemble each sandwich : Spread aïoli on the bottom half of the bread. Lay a few cucumber slices on the aïoli, then place tofu on top of the cucumber slices. (If you're making two large sandwiches, use two pieces of tofu. If you're making four small sandwiches, just use one piece per sandwich.) Top the tofu with some carrot and daikon salad, cilantro, jalapeño, and green onions. Serve immediately. To eat the sandwich later, store it in an airtight container and refrigerate for up to 5 hours. Leftover tofu will keep in an airtight container in the fridge for 4 to 5 days.

PUDDINGS AND CUSTARDS

Crème Brulèe

YIELD: 4 SERVINGS

If you thought that getting just the right texture for classic crème brûlée would be impossible without eggs and cream, this recipe will prove just the opposite! If you don't have a culinary torch (why not?! … they're so much fun), then you can also place these under a broiler set on high for 5 minutes; just watch carefully so that you don't burn the sugar tops.

1 (13.5-ounce) can full-fat coconut milk

1½ cups non dairy milk

1 cup water 1¾ cups sugar

3 tablespoons non dairy margarine

¾ cup cornstarch mixed with ½ cup water

3 tablespoons besan/chickpea flour

1 teaspoon vanilla extract

¾ teaspoon sea salt

2 tablespoons sugar for topping

- Prepare four ramekins by very lightly greasing them with coconut oil or margarine.

- In a 2-quart saucepan, combine the coconut milk, non dairy milk, water, sugar, and margarine and cook over medium heat for about 5 minutes, or until the mixture is hot.

- In a small bowl, mix together the cornstarch slurry, besan, and vanilla extract until very smooth. Add the cornstarch mixture into the coconut milk mixture along with the salt and stir constantly with a whisk over medium heat to let it thicken, which should happen after about 5 minutes.

- Transfer to the prepared ramekins and let cool completely at room temperature until firm. Sprinkle each cup with about ½ tablespoon sugar, then brûlée the tops using a blowtorch. Store in airtight container for up to 1 week in refrigerator.

Chocolate Pudding

YIELD: 2 TO 4 SERVINGS

One of my favorite treats is chocolate pudding. I love how involved it all seems, standing over the stove, meditatively whisking away. This pudding is just as great as other Chocolate Puddings that we know and love with its thick and creamy texture and an unforgettably chocolate flavor.

½ cup cocoa powder

½ cup sugar

2 teaspoons vanilla extract

¼ teaspoon salt

1 cup non dairy milk

3 tablespoons cornstarch

3 tablespoons water

- In a 2-quart saucepan, whisk together the cocoa powder, sugar, vanilla extract, salt, and about ⅓ cup of the non dairy milk. Mix until very smooth with no lumps remaining, and then add in the additional non dairy milk.

- Warm over medium heat. In a small bowl, whisk together the cornstarch and water until no lumps remain. Stir in the cornstarch slurry and keep stirring continuously, over medium heat, until thickened, for about 5 minutes. Transfer to two medium or four small dishes and chill before serving. Store in airtight container for up to 1 week in refrigerator.

Pistachio Pudding

YIELD: 2 TO 4 SERVINGS

This slightly salty and oh-so-sweet treat is easy to bring together and a sure winner for the pistachio lover in your life. I especially love this rich pudding served in small amounts as a dessert or aperitif.

1 cup roasted and salted pistachios, shelled

½ cup granulated sugar

⅓ cup non dairy milk, plus 1½ cups non dairy milk

¼ cup additional granulated sugar

5 tablespoons cornstarch

4 tablespoons water

- In a food processor, pulse the pistachios until crumbly. Add in sugar and blend until powdery—with just a few larger chunks remaining. Add the ⅓ cup nondairy milk and puree until very well combined.

- Transfer pistachio mixture to a 2-quart pot and whisk in the additional nondairy milk and sugar.

- In a small bowl, use a fork to combine the cornstarch and water until no lumps remain. Add this slurry to the pistachio mixture.

- Heat over medium heat, stirring frequently until thickened, for 5 to 7 minutes. Pour into two to four ramekins or serving dishes and let cool completely.

Serve chilled with whipped topping! Store in airtight container for up to 1 week in refrigerator.

Vanilla Plum Rice Pudding

YIELD: 6 SERVINGS

A fragrant take on traditional rice pudding, I like to use basmati for its gorgeous floral notes in addition to the vanilla and plum.

¾ cup basmati or long-grain rice

1½ cups cold water

3 plums, unpeeled, stone removed, and diced

3 teaspoons vanilla extract

½ teaspoon salt

1 cup non dairy milk

½ cup sugar

2 tablespoons sweet white rice flour

¼ cup water

* In a 2- or 3-quart saucepan with a tight-fitting lid, stir together the rice and the cold water. Bring to a boil over medium-high heat. Immediately reduce to a simmer and cover. Do not stir.

* Let simmer for about 20 minutes, or until rice can be fluffed easily with a fork. Increase heat to medium and stir in the plums, vanilla extract, salt, nondairy milk, and sugar. In a smaller bowl, use a fork to stir together the sweet white rice flour and water. Stir the slurry into the rice mixture and cook

for about 5 to 7 minutes, stirring constantly, until thick. Serve warm or cold. Store in airtight container for up to 1 week in refrigerator.

Tapioca Pudding

YIELD: 6 SERVINGS

Tapioca pudding is one of those desserts that most people either love or hate, and I truly do adore it! Having grown up with only the instant puddings, I find this homemade version is so much better. It may change your mind if you're not a fan already. Seek out tapioca pearls in the baking section of most grocery stores, or find an endless variety of shapes and colors in Asian markets.

½ cup small tapioca pearls (not instant)

1 cup canned full-fat coconut milk

2 cups non dairy milk

½ teaspoon salt

½ cup sugar

1 teaspoon vanilla

- In a 2-quart pot, whisk together all the ingredients until smooth. Over medium-high heat, bring to a boil, stirring constantly. Once boiling, reduce heat to low and simmer for 15 minutes, stirring very often, until pudding is thickened and pearls are no longer white and firm but instead clear and gelatinous.

- Place into serving dishes or a flexible airtight container and chill until completely cold. Serve cold. Store in airtight container for up to 1 week in refrigerator.

Fall Harvest Quinoa Pudding

YIELD: 6 SERVINGS

Fruits and fall-time spices combine to make one comforting pudding, and the quinoa gives it a dense, creamy, and chewy texture.

1 tablespoon coconut oil

1 cup chopped pecan pieces

1 apple, chopped into small pieces

½ cup dried dates, chopped

½ teaspoon ground nutmeg

1 teaspoon ground cinnamon

¼ teaspoon cardamom

½ teaspoon salt

½ cup cold non dairy milk

2 teaspoons cornstarch

1 teaspoon vanilla extract

2 cups cooked quinoa

1 cup brown sugar

- Over medium heat, in a 2-quart saucepan, warm the coconut oil until melted. Add the pecans, apples, dates, nutmeg, cinnamon, cardamom, and salt. Continue to cook over medium heat, stirring as to not let the mixture burn. Cook for 3 to 5 minutes, or until apples soften and pecans become fragrant.

- In a small bowl, mix the non dairy milk with the cornstarch and vanilla extract. Whisk together until well combined and no lumps are visible.

- Add the cooked quinoa to the saucepan. Stir in the brown sugar and nondairy milk mixture. Cook over medium heat for about 2 minutes, or until thickened. Serve warm or chilled. Store in airtight container for up to 1 week in refrigerator.

Pumpkin Flan

YIELD: 4 SERVINGS

This is a traditional method of making pumpkin flan, where the pumpkin is allowed to shine on its own, rather than being masked by spices like cinnamon and cloves.

1 cup canned pumpkin or strained pumpkin puree

1 cup non dairy milk

½ cup + 1 tablespoon sugar

¼ teaspoon salt

Dash ground nutmeg

⅓ cup cornstarch

4 tablespoons cold water

- Lightly grease four ramekins or teacups with margarine or cooking spray.

- In a 2-quart saucepan, whisk together the pumpkin, non dairy milk, sugar, salt, and nutmeg until smooth. Warm over medium heat.

- Combine the cornstarch with the cold water and stir until no lumps remain. Drizzle into the pumpkin mixture and continue to whisk, constantly, over medium heat until thickened, for about 7 minutes. You will notice a significant strain on your wrist as it becomes thickened.

- Pour/spoon into lightly greased ramekins and let cool. Transfer to refrigerator and chill completely until cold. Invert onto a small flat plate, or leave in cups for serving. Top with Caramel Sauce. Store in airtight container for up to 1 week in refrigerator.

Cremasicle Custard

YIELD: 4 SERVINGS

This pudding's sunny orange flavor will brighten your day. You can even freeze this pudding in popsicle molds to make creamsicles!

4 tablespoons cornstarch

4 tablespoons cold water

2 cups non dairy milk

½ cup freshly squeezed orange juice

1 cup sugar

1 teaspoon orange zest

½ teaspoon salt

- In small bowl whisk together the cornstarch and cold water and mix well until dissolved. In a small saucepan, combine the non dairy milk, orange juice, and sugar. Stir in the zest and salt. Warm up slightly over medium- low heat, and gradually add in the cornstarch slurry while stirring frequently with a whisk until the mixture reaches a slow boil.

- Reduce heat to low and continue to stir until the mixture becomes thick, for about 10 minutes cooking time total. Divide between four serving dishes and let sit at room temperature until warm. Transfer the dishes to the refrigerator and chill for at least 3 hours, or until it is completely set. Serve chilled. Store in airtight container for up to 1 week in refrigerator.

Tiramisu

YIELD: 10 SERVINGS

Tiramisu is perhaps one of the most popular desserts at Italian restaurants. I always love Tiramisu for its intoxicating fragrance and delightfully melt-in- your-mouth texture. After going gluten-free, I was convinced this dessert would be off limits for good, but no more! Allergy-friendly fancy dessert, at your service.

10 to 12 Ladyfingers

¼ recipe Devilishly Dark Chocolate Sauce

FILLING

1 recipe Mascarpone

1½ cups confectioner's sugar

⅛ teaspoon salt

12 ounces firm silken tofu

3 ounces (about 3 tablespoons) non dairy cream cheese

3 tablespoons cornstarch

4 tablespoons cold water

SAUCE

1 tablespoon cocoa powder, plus more for dusting

1 tablespoon agave

2 tablespoons very strong coffee or espresso

For the Filling

- Place the Mascarpone, confectioner's sugar, salt, tofu, and nondairy cream cheese into a food processor and blend until very smooth, for about 2 minutes. Transfer the mixture into a 2-quart saucepan over medium heat.

- Whisk together the cornstarch and cold water until no lumps remain. Drizzle the cornstarch slurry into the rest of the ingredients and whisk together, continuing to cook over medium heat. Keep stirring continuously until the mixture thickens, for about 5 minutes. Do not walk away from the mixture or it will burn!

- Let cool briefly.

For the Sauce

- Prepare the sauce by whisking together the cocoa powder, agave, and coffee in a small bowl until smooth. **To assemble the Tiramisu**

- In a small, square baking pan, arrange five or six ladyfinger cookies to fit into the pan. Spread the Cocoa Espresso Sauce into a shallow flat dish, big enough for the cookies to lay flat. One by one, dip each side of the cookie into the sauce, briefly, and carefully replace. Repeat until all the cookies have been lightly dipped.

- Divide the Tiramisu filling in half and spread half of the filling on top of the ladyfingers and repeat with one more layer of each. Dust the top with cocoa powder and then drizzle with the Devilishy Dark Chocolate Sauce right before serving. Store in airtight container for up to 3 days in refrigerator.

Brownie Batter Mousse

YIELD: 6 SERVINGS

Tiny bites of chocolate-covered walnuts—that taste a heck of a lot like miniature brownies—speckle this silky mousse, delivering a double dose of chocolate flavor.

6 ounces chopped semi-sweet chocolate

2 tablespoons non dairy milk

1 tablespoon maple syrup

1 cup roughly chopped walnuts

2 (350 g) packages extra-firm silken tofu

1 cup sugar

¾ cup cocoa powder

½ teaspoon salt

1 teaspoon vanilla extract

- Melt the chocolate in a double boiler over low heat until smooth. Stir in the nondairy milk and maple syrup and remove from the heat. Add the walnuts and coat liberally with a thick chocolate layer.

- Line a cookie sheet with a silicone mat or waxed paper. Spread the chocolate-covered walnuts in an even layer on the prepared cookie sheet. Chill the walnuts in your freezer until you are finished making the mousse.

- To make the mousse, simply blend the tofu, sugar, cocoa powder, salt, and vanilla extract in a food processor or blender until extremely smooth, for about 2 minutes, scraping down the sides as needed.

• Remove the chocolate-covered walnuts from the freezer when they are firm and stir them into the mousse. Spoon into individual dishes and serve very cold. Store in airtight container for up to 1 week in refrigerator.

METRIC CONVERSIONS

The recipes in this book have not been tested with metric measurements, so some variations might occur.

Remember that the weight of dry ingredients varies according to the volume or density factor: 1 cup of flour weighs far less than 1 cup of sugar, and 1 tablespoon doesn't necessarily hold 3 teaspoons.

General Formula for Metric Conversion

Ounces to grams   multiply ounces by 28.35

Grams to ounces   multiply ounces by 0.035

Pounds to grams   multiply pounds by 453.5

Pounds to kilograms   multiply pounds by 0.45

Cups to liters   multiply cups by 0.24

Fahrenheit to Celsius   subtract 32 from Fahrenheit

temperature, multiply by 5, divide by 9

Celsius to Fahrenheit   multiply Celsius temperature by 9,

divide by 5, add 32

Volume (Liquid) Measurements

1 teaspoon = ⅙ fluid ounce = 5 milliliters

1 tablespoon = ½ fluid ounce = 15 milliliters 2 tablespoons = 1 fluid ounce = 30 milliliters

¼ cup = 2 fluid ounces = 60 milliliters

⅓ cup = 2⅔ fluid ounces = 79 milliliters

½ cup = 4 fluid ounces = 118 milliliters

1 cup or ½ pint = 8 fluid ounces = 250 milliliters

2 cups or 1 pint = 16 fluid ounces = 500 milliliters

4 cups or 1 quart = 32 fluid ounces = 1,000 milliliters

1 gallon = 4 liters

Oven Temperature Equivalents, Fahrenheit (F) and Celsius (C)

100°F = 38°C

200°F = 95°C

250°F = 120°C

300°F = 150°C

350°F = 180°C

400°F = 205°C

450°F = 230°C

Volume (Dry) Measurements

¼ teaspoon = 1 milliliter

½ teaspoon = 2 milliliters

¾ teaspoon = 4 milliliters 1 teaspoon = 5 milliliters

1 tablespoon = 15 milliliters

¼ cup = 59 milliliters

⅓ cup = 79 milliliters

½ cup = 118 milliliters

⅔ cup = 158 milliliters

¾ cup = 177 milliliters 1 cup = 225 milliliters

4 cups or 1 quart = 1 liter

½ gallon = 2 liters 1 gallon = 4 liters

Linear Measurements

½ in = 1½ cm

1 inch = 2½ cm

6 inches = 15 cm

8 inches = 20 cm

10 inches = 25 cm

12 inches = 30 cm

20 inches = 50 cm

CPSIA information can be obtained
at www.ICGtesting.com
Printed in the USA
BVHW091422030521
606339BV00006B/1128